Le Keux's
Engravings
of
Victorian Cambridge

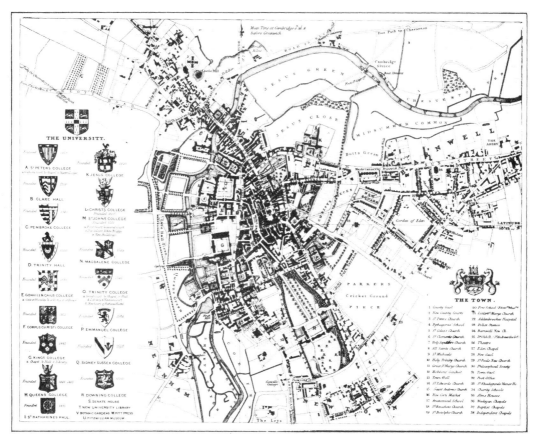

Plan of the University and Town of Cambridge

Le Keux's
Engravings
of
Victorian Cambridge

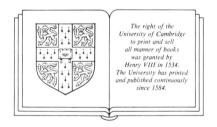

*The right of the
University of Cambridge
to print and sell
all manner of books
was granted by
Henry VIII in 1534.
The University has printed
and published continuously
since 1584.*

Cambridge University Press

Cambridge

London   New York   New Rochelle

Melbourne   Sydney

This book does not include any references to
alumni who graduated after Le Keux's time.

Published by the Press Syndicate of the University of Cambridge
The Pitt Building, Trumpington Street, Cambridge CB2 1RP
32 East 57th Street, New York, NY 10022, USA
10 Stamford Road, Oakleigh, Melbourne 3166, Australia

First published by Granta Editions 1981
First published by Cambridge University Press 1985

Printed in Great Britain at the
University Press, Cambridge

ISBN 0 521 30350 8

Contents

Foreword
by
H.R.H. The Duke of Edinburgh

Originally published in the 1841 edition of John Le Keux's *'Memorials of Cambridge'*, these illustrations appeared at a time when the art of engraving was about to be displaced by photography. The photograph made the engraver's job redundant, but it is thanks to the skilled craftsmanship of the engraver that this record of Victorian Cambridge exists.

The fine engravings reproduced here through the combined efforts of a number of Cambridge-based companies and their employees will raise money in aid of the Addenbrooke's Hospital Cancer Scanning Appeal Fund, a fund created to make the most advanced technology in medical use available to those who need it.

Every element of this volume has been donated free of charge by the companies involved, from the initial idea through to the sale over the counter to you. This represents a splendid co-operative effort by the book business fraternity of Cambridge, and I hope it achieves the success it deserves.

Acknowledgements

This book is the product of the generosity of those individuals and companies whose efforts have combined in aid of the Addenbrooke's Hospital Cancer Scanning Appeal Fund. There can be no order of merit; this book is entirely the sum of its parts with each part being essential and freely given.

Thanks are due to H.R.H. The Duke of Edinburgh for the Foreword and L. P. Wilkinson for the text: Colin Walsh of Book Production Consultants for the original idea: The Cambridgeshire Collection, Central Library, Cambridge for supplying the original etchings: Ron Jones for initial design consultations: Jim Reader of Book Production Consultants for text and jacket design: Sue Latham of Book Production Consultants for organising and co-ordinating the project: Cambridge Litho (Plates) Ltd. for camera origination, bromides and film: Bowaters and William Guppy & Son Ltd. for supplying the text paper, Nimrod Matt Art 115 g/m^2: King's English for typesetting and supplying repro: the staff and management of The Burlington Press for printing the text: Sebastian Carter of The Rampant Lions Press for designing and printing the endpapers: the staff and management of Cambridge University Press for supplying binding materials and binding production: Foister and Jagg Ltd for supplying and printing the jackets: Patrick Stephens Ltd for warehousing facilities: Bowes and Bowes Booksellers, Heffers Booksellers, King's College Chapel Bookstore and Mowbray's Bookshop for the sale of the books: The Cambridge Evening News for promotion: and Granta Editions for conceiving the complete project.

This acknowledgement is for the first Printing only.

Cambridge Town

The Cambridge of 1860, apart from the Colleges and University, was a town whose medieval origins were characterized by its churches. The oldest of these was St Bene't's with its pre-Conquest tower. In the centre of the town Great St Mary's rose, a fine example of East Anglian Perpendicular. This was surrounded by the smaller churches: All Saints, St Clement's, St Michael's, St Edward's, St Botolph's and Holy Trinity. All of these buildings showed where dry land had once risen above the marshy fenland.

Cambridge was famous for its "Stourbridge Fair", the largest in England, if not in Europe. It was held in the fields beyond Barnwell Priory between the river. However, this site gradually became deserted when the railways made such fairs superfluous; now all that is left to serve as a reminder is the little street named "Garlic Row" and the Norman Leper chapel.

There was a violent contrast between the squalid little town and the fine colleges. Before 1800 the population of Cambridge never reached five figures. The streets were filthy and the boundary – "The King's Ditch" – was an open sewer, blamed for the pestilences which, down to 1665, frequently dispersed the scholars. However, in 1610 Town and Gown combined to lead the "New River" from Nine Wells; at this time the riparian Colleges joined together and canalized the Cam to create "The Backs". The University has always had an influence on the town; it intervened and prevented the railway station and consequent new development from spoiling the beauty of "The Backs" and the historic centre.

It was inevitable that Town and Gown should clash, and clash they did, violently in the Middle Ages and spasmodically also thereafter. The University blamed the Borough for not cleansing the streets and the Ditch, and the tradesmen and lodging-house keepers were maligned for profiteering. However, the burden of the grievance was on the other side. The students, who arrived in about 1200, were no less contumelious here than elsewhere, while the townsmen were jealous of the academic privileges especially when the well-endowed colleges arose amidst the relative squalor of the town.

In the Civil War the Town was Parliamentarian, the Colleges mostly Royalist. However, by 1860 both Borough and University had submitted to reform, and in that atmosphere the University tacitly abandoned most of its peculiar privileges. In 1855 all matters of dispute were amicably settled through an arbitrator.

The New Church, Barnwell

Cambridge from Castle Hill

Cambridge from the Ely Road

14

The Castle

The Fitzwilliam Museum

The Market Place, showing the Town Hall and Hobsons Conduit

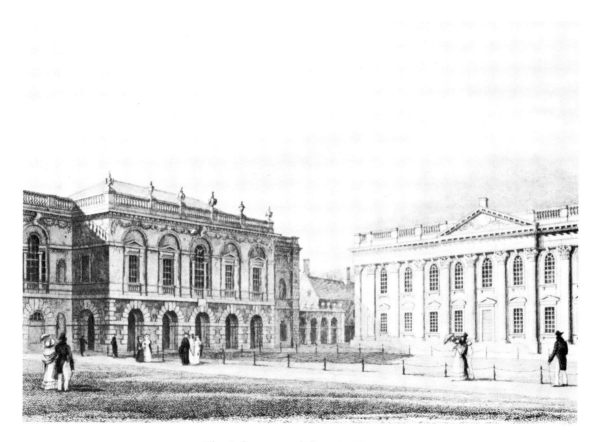

The Library and Senate House

The interior of the Senate House

The University Press Building

A view showing All Saints Church

St. Andrew's Church

The interior of St. Bene't's Church

St. Botolph's Church

The interior of St. Botolph's Church

St. Clement's Church

Great St. Mary's Church

The interior of Great St. Mary's Church

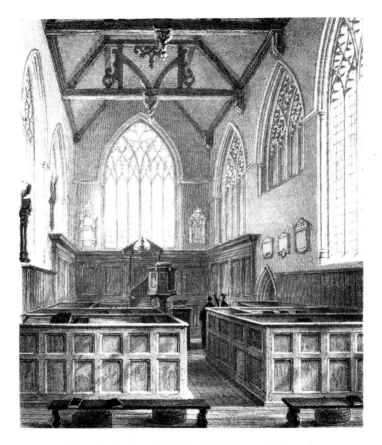

The interior of Little St. Mary's Church

St. Michael's Church

The interior of St. Sepulchre's Church

The interior of St. Sepulchre's Church

Trinity Church

Christ's College

Founded in 1505

Lady Margaret Beaufort, mother of Henry VII, prompted by her confessor, John Fisher, refounded William Bingham's small college called God's House and renamed it Christ's College in 1505. To enter Lady Margaret's court you pass through a richly heraldic gate with her coat of arms above the archway. The whole court had to be refaced in the 18th century because of its bad repair. The Master's Lodge, which is situated between the Chapel and the Hall, had a first floor suite which was designed for Lady Margaret's frequent visits to the College. In 1640–42, when the numbers had risen to 160, an unknown architect built Fellows' Building, a landmark in Cambridge architecture. Free-standing, away from the court and beside the garden, the building is eleven bays long and three storeys high. It is classical in style but has traces of Jacobean features. The windows, with one vertical mullion and one horizontal transom, were the first of their kind in Cambridge. The college garden boasted of many fine trees and shrubs; it was particularly noted for its fine mulberry trees, which can be attributed to James I, who encouraged the production of silkworms.

After the middle of the seventeenth century Christ's declined; before this time it had as members men such as Leland the antiquarian and the poet Francis Quarles; and in 1625 Milton entered the college. In the beginning of the nineteenth century the College started to prosper again. Charles Darwin entered in 1827.

Christ's College

The First Court, Christ's College

The Second Court, Christ's College

Tree Court, Christ's College

Clare College

Founded in 1326

In 1326, a generation after Hugh de Balsham had founded Peterhouse, some members of the still emergent University attempted to found a college of its own, like the one that still exists in Oxford. This would have failed, had it not been adopted in 1338 by Elizabeth de Burgh, Lady of Clare.

Nothing remains of the original buildings; instead Clare Hall (called 'Clare College' since 1856) acquired a noble square renaissance palace. It consisted mainly of seventeenth century buildings but it was completed in the eighteenth century when balustrades replaced the battlements, arched windows were squared off, and the small but elegant Chapel was built out eastwards. The elaborate eastern entrance, where Tudor features of oriel, niches and fan vault are blended with a renaissance arch, is very attractive. The monumental river-front clearly shows Wren's impact on Cambridge architects. Clare possesses the famous three-arched bridge which was the first of the stone river-bridges; built in 1640, it is decorated with balustrades surmounted by orbs. From King's bridge Clare completes a superb composition with King's Chapel and Gibbs's Building beyond the river and great lawn.

In its middle years Clare harboured some notable divines such as Hugh Latimer the Protestant martyr, Ralph Cudworth the Platonist (imported from Emmanuel in 1685 as Master), and the future Archbishop Tillotson.

Clare Hall

Clare Hall from the Gardens

The interior of the chapel, Clare Hall

The Quadrangle, Clare Hall

Corpus Christi College

Founded in 1352

Corpus Christi is unique among Cambridge and Oxford Colleges as it was not founded by an individual, but by two town guilds of merchants, the Guild of Corpus Christi and the Guild of the Blessed Virgin Mary. The College was situated near St Bene't's Church and used this as its place of worship.

The Old Court is our best specimen of an early medieval college, primitive indeed behind the later buttresses and plaster facing. In 1823 it was elbowed aside by what amounted to a new college, built on the south side by William Wilkins in an imposing, if uninspired, neo-Gothic style. Corpus has remained a comparatively small, intimate society, like Peterhouse or Magdalene.

Its collection of plate has many splendid pieces, including a drinking horn even older than the College. Many of these were given by Archbishop Parker, who had been Master from 1544 to 1552. He also bequeathed to the Library 433 volumes, one of the finest collections of Anglo-Saxon and other medieval manuscripts. The Library possesses many early printed books gathered from the dispersed libraries of monasteries dissolved under Henry VIII. Its Canterbury Gospels, reputedly used by St Augustine, are lent to Canterbury for the enthronement ceremony of its Archbishops.

The dramatic poets Marlowe and Fletcher resided at Corpus Christi.

Corpus Christi College

Corpus Christi College and St. Botolph's Church

The interior of Corpus Christi College Chapel

The Quadrangle, Corpus Christi College

Downing College

Founded in 1800

Sir George Downing died in 1749 but, owing to litigation, the College resulting from his will was not chartered until 1800. The winning architectural design by William Wilkins, in neo-Grecian style, envisaged a campus with buildings on four sides of a huge lawn, but this proved too ambitious for the endowment. Only the temple-like Hall and Master's Lodge, with a range running north from each, were built. The intended *Propylaea* on the north side, and the Chapel and Library on the south, never materialized. Only twenty sets of rooms out of the planned fifty were built. The land along Downing Street, where the intended entrance avenue should have been, out of necessity was sold to the University as a site for laboratories.

Financial difficulties also crippled the original constitution conceived by Pitt. Its waiving of celibacy, and of the Holy Orders except for the two tutors, remained as influential precedents within the University. Unfortunately endowments sufficed for three only of the fourteen Fellowships, all to be in Law or Medicine with the tenure limited to twelve years. To make money, well-to-do 'pensioners' had to be admitted without restriction of subject. So Downing became an ordinary college, poor but spacious, dreaming of the completion of Wilkins's classic design.

The interior of the Hall, Downing College

A proposed view of Downing College, 1842

Emmanuel College

Founded in 1584

Emmanuel College, established in 1584 for the training of preachers, was the first Protestant foundation in Cambridge. It was founded by Sir Walter Mildmay, a Christ's man. For fifty years it rose on the tide of Puritanism. It contributed numerous emigrants to New England, among them John Harvard, who died at the age of thirty-one, but who like Mildmay 'set an acorn', by his will. In Carolingian times its 'Cambridge Platonists' – Whichcote, Tuckney, Sterry, Cudworth, Culverwell, John Smith, four of whom became Heads of colleges – threw off Puritan narrowness and contempt for reason and learning. After the Restoration a royalist Master, William Sancroft (later Archbishop), led a reaction against the Low Church ethos for which Emmanuel had become famous.

Probably through William Sancroft the building of a new Chapel was entrusted to Wren, who set it in a long colonade with a picture gallery above. The original court, embodying relics of an old Dominican friary, was open on the side of Emmanuel Street, where the main gate stood. You now enter the College from St Andrew's Street and are immediately confronted by Wren's mildly baroque composition. Emmanuel possesses some lovely spacious grounds, including a small lake. The College also owns a fine collection of plate.

Emmanuel College

Emmanuel College Chapel

Gonville and Caius College

Founded in 1384 and 1557

The Norfolk cleric Edmund Gonville's provision of 1348 for founding a college was fulfilled posthumously in 1351 by William Bateman on a site near his own new foundation of Trinity Hall. Gonville Hall was a modest affair, markedly East Anglian, until John Keys, who had previously attended as a student, obtained a royal charter in 1557 and founded Gonville and Caius. Following a scholarly fashion John Keys had Latinised his name as 'Caius'. A Tudor court physician of European reputation, he studied medicine at the famous Italian University of Padua. When he returned, he introduced to the British medical world many revolutionary ideas.

Caius, whose imposing tomb lies in the Chapel, built his court southwards from Gonville Court.

One side, on the south, consists only of a wall with the Gate of Honour inserted; such open plans were a novelty introduced from France. Caius' Gates of Humility, Virtue and Honour are fantasies symbolising the progress of students through his College. The classical style of the Gates of Virtue and Honour is untypical of English architecture of the mid-sixteenth century. The Gate of Humility was moved to the Master's garden when Waterhouse enclosed Tree Court with a building whose tower dwarfs Gibbs's neighbouring Senate House, but this occurred just after Le Keux.

Caius College is still distinguished for John Caius' speciality – medicine. Many famous physicians have studied at Caius, among them, William Harvey, who discovered the circulation of blood.

Gonville and Caius College from the street

Gonville and Caius College from the Fellows' Garden

The interior of Gonville and Caius College Chapel

The Gate of Honour, Gonville and Caius College

Jesus College

Founded in 1496

Jesus College is peculiar in its secluded situation, its retention of monastic buildings, and the spaciousness of its grounds, which are sufficient to accommodate all its playing fields. The College was founded in 1496 by Bishop Alcock of Ely. The site had once been a prosperous convent but, at the time of the foundation of the College, it only housed two nuns, one of them disreputable.

The impression of seclusion is emphasized by the approach. A long paved walk between high walls leads to Alcock's gate-tower. The cloistered court of the convent to the right (its yellow brick arches date only from 1773) is shadowed by the Chapel. Although the north and south aisles and part of the nave were demolished, it still remains a venerable building. It is mainly thirteenth-century Gothic in style, though many Norman features survive. The chancel is particularly fine, the east end having been reconstructed in 1849–53 by Pugin, who filled its high lancet windows with passable imitations of Chartres glass. Throughout the College you see the rebus of Alcock, a cockerel standing on a globe. Alcock was responsible for the transformation of the refectory above the kitchens, which is now the Hall. It possesses a very fine chestnut roof.

Among the many distinguished students who have attended Jesus College were Thomas Cranmer, Laurence Sterne, Samuel Taylor Coleridge and Thomas Robert Malthus.

Jesus College from the meadows

The interior of Jesus College Chapel

King's College

Founded in 1441

King's College, founded by Henry VI in 1441 in conjunction with his school at Eton, is most famous for its Chapel. The Founder's statutes fixed the society at a total of seventy Etonian Fellows and Scholars and this remained the same until 1861.

Often delayed by civil war or financial stringency, but never abandoned by Henry's successors, the Chapel was completed in 1515 with Tudor magnificence. Its chief interior glories are the fan vault, the unrivalled set of early Renaissance windows (of Flemish inspiration), and the rood screen, probably the work of Italian carvers, surmounted since the seventeenth century by the organ. The famous choir was also instituted by the Founder. King Henry envisaged a great court south of the Chapel, but this was only begun in 1724, with James Gibbs's serenely dignified Fellows' Building looking both ways over spacious lawns. The court was only completed in 1828 by Wilkins's successfully daring neo-Gothic screen with the Gate-lodge along King's Parade. He also built the Hall towards the river. Only then was the cramped Old Court north of the Chapel (temporary for 380 years) evacuated.

Kingsmen include Sir Francis Walsingham, General Monck, Sir Robert Walpole and his son Horace, 'Turnip' Townshend and Charles Simeon.

The front of King's College

The Fellows' Building and Provost's Lodge, King's College

The interior of the Hall, King's College

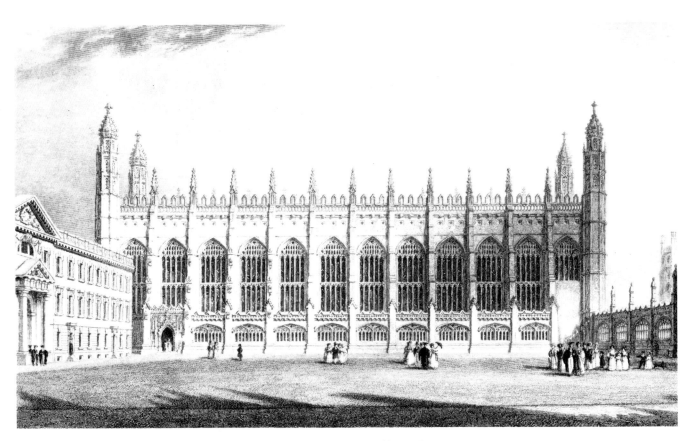

King's College Chapel

The interior of King's College Chapel

The Old Court, King's College

King's College Library

King's College

Magdalene College

Founded in 1542

In 1428 Henry VI authorised a hostel, soon named Buckingham College, for Benedictine students from the Fenland abbeys. After the suppression of monastries, in 1542, Thomas Lord Audley of Walden took over the court containing its Chapel and Hall (made of clunch and faced with red brick), and founded Magdalene College. The owner of the Walden Estate at Audley End is known as 'The Visitor' and always nominates the Master of the College. Lord Braybrooke in 1813 nominated his son George, aged twenty-four, who ruled for forty years. Nevile and Clayton, who as Masters built Trinity Great Court and St John's Second Court respectively, had been successive Masters of Magdalene.

Magdalene was prominent in the movement towards earnestness that began in the seventeen-eighties. Evangelicals were entrusted to its Tutor, William Farish, by the Clapham Sect and the Ellard Society. The College was always poor, but in the eighteenth century a handsome building just north of the Hall was erected. The date in its superscription, 1724, refers to its later reception of Magdalene's great treasure, the library of three thousand volumes bequeathed in 1703 by Samuel Pepys. He was formerly a student of the College and gave his prints, his diary in shorthand and eleven red oak bookcases. The College was noted for its tea-drinking. Its chief Victorian ornament was Charles Kingsley.

Magdalene College

The Pepys Library, Magdalene College

Pembroke College

Founded in 1347

Marie de St Paul, Countess of Pembroke, was a friend of the Lady of Clare, and followed her lead by founding Pembroke College in 1347. Students of her native France were to have preference, a unique provision.

The original façade is discernible behind the ashlar facing of 1712. The seventeenth century saw important developments. Two ranges were built out eastwards from the Hall. Then in 1663 a new Chapel was added on the south side of the Old Court. Given by Matthew Wren, Bishop of Ely, this was the first architectural venture of his brilliant nephew, then aged thirty-one and at that time Professor of Astronomy at Oxford. It was one of the first churches in England and the earliest building in Cambridge to display a pure classical style. The old Chapel on the north-west corner of the court was converted into a library and embellished with an enchanting plaster ceiling. In Le Keux's time the Hall, Library and other buildings had not been ousted or overshadowed by the pretentious red-brick buildings of Alfred Waterhouse in the French neo-Gothic style.

The original buildings housed distinguished poets such as Spenser, Crashaw, Smart and Gray (a refugee from Peterhouse). Also divines such as Ridley, Whitgift and Andrewes; and the younger Pitt (who within a few years of his leaving Pembroke was Prime Minister).

Pembroke College from the street

Pembroke College Hall

The interior of the chapel, Pembroke College

The interior of the Hall, Pembroke College

Peterhouse

Founded in 1284

Towards the end of the thirteenth century the collegiate system was taking shape at Oxford, to rescue scholars of the University from the temptations of the town and the rapacity of lodging-house keepers. In 1284 Hugh de Balsham, Bishop of Ely, inaugurated a similar system at Cambridge. Adapting the ideas of the Oxford man Walter de Merton, he amalgamated two houses he had previously acquired for secular scholars and founded Peterhouse. It was to be financed by tithes from the neighbouring church of St Peter-without-Trumpington-Gate (predecessor of Little St Mary's 1340–52).

Traces remain of the Hall built in 1286, but the College acquired its present appearance mainly in the seventeenth-eighteenth centuries. The Chapel built in 1632 is a remarkable blend of Gothic and Renaissance features, having a fine ceiling and an east window based on a design by Rubens. The aspect of the main court is of eighteenth century ashlar facing surrounding large sash windows, which were imposed by the gifted amateur architect, Sir James Burrough, later Master of Caius. He also designed the elegant Palladian extension eastwards on the north side to the street.

Le Keux's engravings just antedate the new look given to the Hall and Combination Room by Sir G. Scott and some Pre-Raphaelite artists.

Alumni of Peterhouse include Lord Kelvin and the poet Thomas Gray before he moved on to Pembroke.

Peterhouse

Peterhouse Chapel

Gisborne Court, Peterhouse

Gisbrook Court, Peterhouse

Queens' College

Founded in 1448

Queens' College was founded in 1448 by Andrew Docket, who guided it as President for over forty years. It was patronised first by Margaret of Anjou, Queen of Henry VI. Her former lady-in-waiting, Elizabeth Woodville, Queen of Henry's supplanter Edward IV, continued the patronage of the College thus known as "Queens'".

It presents the most complete example of a late medieval college in Cambridge. The architect of its gate-tower and Principal Court, all faced with red brick, was probably Reginald Ely, first master mason of King's Chapel. Beyond the Hall is the small, irregular Cloister Court. Its western range of red brick is washed by the river and pierced to give access to the Mathematical Bridge of 1749. The timber-structured bridge was cleverly designed so as to need no support in the form of nails. Queens' President's Lodge has a gallery attached which forms the northern range of Cloister Court, the only timber-framed Tudor building to be seen in any Cambridge College and delightfully picturesque. A plain, but not inelegant, white brick building by Essex (1756) forms the south-west corner of the College.

The external gable and turret in the south-west corner of the Principal Court housed the humanist scholar Erasmus in the beginning of the sixteenth century (he is said to have complained bitterly about the damp, cold Cambridge weather). Erasmus helped to introduce Greek and printing to Cambridge.

The entrance gateway, Queens' College

The Great Court, Queens' College

The Second Court, Queens' College

Walnut Tree Court, Queens' College

The interior of the Hall, Queens' College

The Mathematical Bridge, Queens' College

St. Catharine's College

Founded in 1473

In 1473, Robert Wodelarke, Provost of King's College, where he was also Henry VI's Master of Works, founded what was then known as Catharine Hall. it faced onto Queens' Lane (formerly Milne Street).

After impoverished beginnings it had, by 1675, 150 students and was fifth in size amongst the colleges.

Matthew Scrivener, Vicar of Haslingfield and a Catharine man, initiated a new building programme. This operation was placed in the hands of Robert Grumbold, an admirable local master mason, who was working on a building project at Clare College at the same time. At St Catharine's a large red brick quadrangle was started by Grumbold and continued by James Essex. In 1557 it was decided to leave one side open, as in Caius Court and Sidney Sussex. The east side, therefore, opened onto Trumpington Street, so that the college then faced about; handsome gates were erected and a grove was planted on that side. By Le Keux's time, however, St Catharine's had for some reason declined, and its future recovery could hardly have been foreseen.

Among its earlier members were John Bradford, the Reformist martyr; Whitgift, who later moved to Pembroke; and Shirley, the dramatic poet.

St. Catharine's College

The interior of the chapel, St. Catharine's College

St. John's College

Founded in 1511

John Fisher, as executor to Lady Margaret Beaufort, established in 1511 her college of St John's. It flourished, but not entirely in line with their pious aim. By admitting wealthy Fellow Commoners it became by 1606 'not inferior to any college for the bringing up of young gentlemen'. While it fostered the new learning, and later the new puritanism, it became part of the Tudor and Stuart system of patronage. St John's was overtaken in distinction by Trinity, its only rival in numbers. The College declined somewhat after the Restoration, when it became the chief High Church and Tory college.

To enter the First Court you pass through a splendid heraldic gate-tower which has Lady Margaret's coat of arms over the gate-way; a second court with a complementary tower was added in 1598–1602. The third court, completed in 1671, reaches the river. In 1831 the 'Bridge of Sighs' was built and connected the original old buildings with the neo-Gothic New Court, a romantic screen to the 'Backs' on the north side.

St John's alumni include statesmen such as the Cecils, Strafford, Fairfax, Castlereagh, Wilberforce and Palmerston. Scholars include Cheke, Ascham, Bentley, Herschel, and poets include Wyatt, Green, Nashe, Herrick, Prior and Wordsworth.

St. John's College Gateway

The Second Court, St. John's College

The interior of the chapel, St. John's College

The Bridge of Sighs, St. John's College

The New Buildings, St. John's College

The New Buildings, St. John's College, from the gardens

Sidney Sussex College

Founded in 1596

Sidney Sussex College occupies the site of the chief monastic establishment of Medieval Cambridge, that of the Franciscan Grey Friars. After its dissolution in 1538 its buildings were acquired by Trinity College as a quarry for their Chapel, and it was only under pressure from Archbishop Whitgift, formerly their own Master, that Trinity surrendered the site. Whitgift was the executor to Lady Frances Sidney, Countess of Sussex. She was married to the Earl who figures as Robert Dudley's rival in Scott's "Kenilworth". The College was named after her and founded in 1596, the second (after Emmanuel) of the Protestant foundations. It was the first college to allow Scotsmen and Irishmen to become Fellows.

Between 1821 and 1832 the buildings were much altered and spoilt by Jeffry Wyatt (Sir Jeffry Wyatville). He introduced pseudo-Elizabethan features, cased the walls of rich red brick in cement, and built the present gate-tower of stone.

The College possesses one of the loveliest gardens in Cambridge, some fine silver and three portraits of Oliver Cromwell, who entered the college in 1616, when it was still in its infancy, but left after a year without a degree on the death of his father.

Sidney Sussex College

Sidney Sussex College

The Interior of the Hall, Sidney Sussex College

Sidney Sussex College from the Master's Garden

Trinity College

Founded in 1546

Trinity College is the largest, richest and greatest of the Cambridge and Oxford Colleges. It was founded by Henry VIII in 1546, for a Master and sixty Fellows. Henry VIII's designs, which united two earlier foundations, King's Hall and Michaelhouse, were carried out through the reign of Elizabeth.

In 1597–1605, the Master of the College, Thomas Nevile, re-designed Great Court, centred on its fountain. At his own expense he built the Hall, based on the Middle Temple, in Gothic style, splendid in its spaciousness. He built out westwards from the Hall towards the river a colonnaded court (Nevile's Court) in the Renaissance style. This court is closed by the library built by Wren, inspired by Sansovino's at Venice but using for functional purposes certain features of construction more reminiscent of French baroque. The bookshelves and decoration of the library were carved by Grinling Gibbons and are worthy of the noble collection it houses.

Rivalled only by St John's in the number of students it admits, Trinity is unequalled for the number of eminent and distinguished names, including Bacon, Newton, Barrow, Dryden, Byron, Tennyson, Thackeray, Macaulay, Bentley and Porson – to mention only a few of those who attended the College before the time of Le Keux.

The Great Court, Trinity College

Trinity College Hall

Trinity College Hall, viewed from the cloisters

The Wren Library, Trinity College

The Interior of the Wren Library, Trinity College

King's Court, Trinity College

Statue of Sir Isaac Newton, Trinity College

Trinity College from the River Cam

Trinity Hall

Founded in 1350

Trinity Hall retains its original title despite the founding of Trinity College: there is no connection. It was founded in 1350 by William Bateman, Bishop of Norwich. The College Chapel, though not consecrated till 1513, was the earliest to be licensed for a college, just anticipating those of Gonville (the first actually built) and Pembroke. Previously to this each college worshipped at some neighbouring church. Bateman's enthusiasm was for law and Trinity Hall has always been famous for lawyers, producing notable judges such as Cockburn L. C. J. Right from the beginning its Fellows in Civil Law could be laymen. It had links with the great world. Endowed for comparative comfort, it was enriched by successive gifts of magnificent plate, still intact. Hunting has always been one of "The Hall"'s characteristic recreations.

The Principal Court whose east side was remodelled in 1852 by Anthony Salvin after damage by fire, was faced with ashlar in the eighteenth century by Sir James Burrough and makes a peaceful and dignified impression. Jutting out beyond it, towards the river, is the step-gabled Library, which is Elizabethan. The Library has a remarkable interior consisting of Jacobean seats and bookcases where the books were actually chained to the cases to prevent theft.

Lord Chesterfield (of the Letters) and Lord Fitzwilliam (of the Museum) were Hall men; also Tusser the agriculturalist and Holinshed the chronicler in early times, and those fine Victorians F. D. Maurice and Leslie Stephen.

Trinity Hall

Trinity Hall from the garden